SANDBOX

Also by Michael R. Lane

Poetry
A Drop of Midnight
Mortal Thoughts
Love & Sensuality
A Leap Year of Haiku

Fiction
Emancipation
UFOs and God
The Family Stone
Long Journey Home
Exchange Student

C. J. Cavanaugh Mysteries
The Gem Connection
Blue Sun
The Gem Connection
Six Weeks

SANDBOX

~Poems~

Michael R. Lane

BARE BONES PRESS
P.O. Box 9653, Seattle, WA 98109

Published by Bare Bones Press, Seattle, Washington.

Design: Bare Bones Press
Production: Bare Bones Press
Cover Art: Monika Younger

Bare Bones Press
P.O. Box 9653
Seattle, WA 98109

www.michaelrlane.com
www.barebonespress.com

Second Edition: September 2023

*To the language spirits of an art
that knows no bounds.*

POET'S NOTE

The language for the Second Edition of *Sandbox* is identical to the First Edition. Poetic forms for some poems have been modified from their original publication to better suit the poet's intended cadence.

Contents

SANDBOX

Plain INsights

I am not a professor of literature.
I am not a teacher of creative writing.
As a wordsmith, I find myself limited
to express what I can in hopes of art.
My history lists no significant awards of merit,
no fellowships, grants, MFAs or contest victories.
Still, passion and fervor burn deep inside of me
shoving me onward to observe each glint
and twinkle and burst and sparkle
of those ambient, brilliant hot shining stars
known commonly as inspiration.
I follow the universe.
I reach not to hold.
I empty myself of all expectations,
surrendering to the wanton will of The Muse.
My purpose is simple,
as are often my words:
to share plain insights with you.

Blank Pages

I hold before me a blank page

(my mind)

its gray self-unraveling itself

(in time)

distilling rational intellection

(wonders)

diluting not one saline drop

(sublime)

From fossiliferous crust evolves polished gems

(as truth)

which liberate each day in every way

(I chose)

pure thought, instinctually refined

(introspection)

immix with sepia questions

(connection)

Mystical origins radiate ideas

                        (one body)

stimulating matter across electronic spheres

                        (one world)

diverse parts of a central sum

                        (one universe)

I hold within me a vacant page

                        (my mind)

The Question Is

The question is
    a badgering of words
or word
    spoken for purposes
of disclosing
    previously unwarranted
information
    which at the time
may seem significant
    to the inquirer
regardless of
    importance
or lack thereof
    in the overall
scheme of things
    conjured up in
the colossal form
    of consecutive
        insurmountable
            whys

to which
    my overzealous responses
seldom satisfy
    the both of us.

The Screen

I watch the screen —
green letters and digits on a baser green —
mind in limbo.
How to reenter the world?
comfort portal?
love slide?
fear maze?
pain funnel?
future probe?
— yes, future probe.
Specific focus: mankind.

I watch the screen —
green on a baser green.

Whirlpool

Our lives,
like pages of a calendar,
are numbered;
swept away
in the swirling,
constant
whirlpool of time
spiraling upward,
forever onward,
into oblivious,
shadowed worlds entwined,
drowning out,
with pain-filled,
weighted sighs.

The Nature of Dust (Form 1)

When moisture vacates
soil once rich and fertile
its particles defy gravity
play upon the whims of air
tickle ambient rays of sunlight
aligning themselves with
electromagnetic charges
of any solid, liquid or gas.

The Nature of Dust (Form 2)

A cloud bowl of burden
brimming with dead skin cells
and seasoned with withered flesh —
greedy dust mites feast
growing plump and sluggish
on what healthy lungs expel
as mucous particles into the air
that comes to rest on level surfaces.

The Nature of Dust (Form 3)

The Great Equalizer of low caste and high
ferments human remains of kind and evil.
Symbolic rituals entrenched in antiquated time
mesh with religious provisions of final farewells
from incinerating sun high to watery moon set
vessels ceremonially cremated by eternal flames.
Flesh, skin and bones cede to mother earth;
spirits liberated to play in their birth universe.

The Nature of Dust (Form 4)

Death did not silently creep into his nest:
it nibbled and gnawed at his ordained flesh,
a constant decay measured in agony and joy —
a banquet time had given, then taken away.
Once death had voraciously snacked on his body
his spirit succumbed to its insatiable craving,
his vapid remains housed in a wooden casket –
human compost fated to enrich hallowed ground.

The Nature of Dust (Form 5)

Pneumonoultramicroscopicsilicovolcanokoniosis
Black, Brown, Labrador and Popcorn workers' lungs,
diseases few that infiltrate
spongy recesses of respiratory organs
affecting and infecting an averse host
oblivious of its diabolical effect
of robbing sacred beings of precious breath —
such is the random wanton nature of dust.

Junkie

It cost him another dream today,
utopian placebo
crushed
then boiled,
curdling his blood,
turning his mind to cottage cheese,
on the edge of a dull sleep,
terrified of a world
too real,
too deadly,
for him.

Blood and Vinegar

We impart to each other
derogatory lies regarding
other races or cultures,
espousing superiority,
attempting to justify
the annihilation of one another;

foolish beliefs,

lethal outcomes.

Time

Peering skyward remembering sunlight,
intimate stars yawn and wink;
royal blue canvas eclipsing daylight
contour the horizon where twilight meet.

Intimate stars yawn and wink
angel dust of human kind;
contour the horizon where twilight meet
silent pulses of timed heartbeats.

Angel dust of human kind,
salt sea breezes prick live flesh,
silent pulses of timed heartbeats;
blind visionary's universe aligns.

Salt sea breezes prick live flesh,
royal blue canvas eclipsing daylight —
blind visionary's universe aligns
peering skyward, remembering sunlight.

To Kiss a Moment

What is it like
to kiss a moment?

Does it tingle upon the lips,
does it bite the fleshy tongue —
moan throaty pleasure's bliss
or blend two hearts as one?

Has it power unencumbered
to release orgasmic winds
and awaken that which slumbers
at the apex of all men?

Then there is the space of change.

Does time greet the splendid moment;
grip firm each shivering hand,
ask for trust and atonement
as it uproots it from its land?

Is it then that we love a moment;
is it when gray fades to black
like ourselves and all about us
that we find moments born to die?

Blink

In a pupil that twinkles,
        existence,
an ant discovers a crumb of bread
        a seed sprouts
wind dances over water
        sunshine crackles against rock
clouds chase a dream
        rain nourishes and cleanses
turkeys drown
        a grasshopper stills
before a praying mantis
        in grass as high
as a child's bare ankle
        who runs by both
to catch a baseball
        thrown by her friend,
before the blink
        that will blind the eye
of our universe.

Still We Laugh

The skipping stone propels along spineless mountain jewels
swaying in sand winds blown from beach to desert to beach.
Cursed blue skies phantom thunder dancers atop boulders
prancing, clawing, praising
the acrid scent of wonder.
A fern blade rises erect and stills the growing grass between
bare-prints embossed in shattered fields of glass.
Fire towers crowned by paper lace assailed by wingless gliders
sting the succulent pulp of a crimson heart.

Still we laugh.

Sanctions against Humanity

Blackbirds caged beneath our purple canopy of dusk,
iron feathered prey of economic carnivores.
Sculpted humans from metallic flesh,
muscled by techno-fibers,
driven by silicone hearts.
Fanatical paranoids wag manicured fingers:
"Not responsible are we," they retort.
"Criminals are born and jobs are available,
paying minimum wages for life support."
Shuttle sputters at peak trajectory,
freezes,
nosedives,
tumbles and rolls,
crashing home without a whisper
into the throat of a manic scream.

Evolution Comes First

Behind the diaphanous drapes of dreams myriad questions rummage through our infinite, eternal spirits, playing out through the subconscious of our conditioned minds. Pitted fears, harassing doubts, insurgent tribal instincts, and nettled thoughts prick pinholes of light through the shear drapes to spot our conscious floor with dust mite clues of who we are and what we seek. Night has a mystic clasp on our human psyche like none other in the realm of nature. It dredges up our primordial ghosts; reminds us that before we walked upright, before the gift of fire, we were primates evolving toward a Neanderthal ancestry.

       How simple the formula.

       How genetic the blueprint.

       Neither technology, science, religion, art, language, intellectual development nor all other achievements of modern humankind have loosened the talon grip of night. Disrupt our creature comforts, limit our food and water supply, and fear is injected back into our veins. We leap backwards to become those same frightened creatures who struggled to survive in a world teeming with life attempting to do the same.

Natural Evolution

The space of time spreads over
forests and deserts and islands
and swamps and tundra and mountains
and oceans and lakes and rivers
and seas.

In its bounty are fish and fowl
and insects and mammals and birds
and peace.
And in its eyes exist
no images of man.

MODERN Definitions

Sincerity: dew steamed mist by the gluttonous
                  flames of selfishness.

Compassion: small fish floundering in the sun
                  blind sea of apathy.

Understanding: murky tears tracing the woeful
                  cheek of willful ignorance.

Hope: beggar children incarcerated beneath
                  a dull iron blanket of cruelty.

People: weary demented creatures wandering
                  society's derisive maze.

Fantasy: a claim that all is possible in our
                  borrowed world.

This Is How We Die

Instinctively we are
fascinated as youths,
haunted as elders,
shuddering
when acid lips
encircle fertile hearts
sucking
nibbling
digesting flesh with raspy praise.

Efficacious beast,
we deny
repress
dismiss
as light rejects darkness
illusion dispels reality
sorrow purges joy.

Imminent forces prevail.
Earthly time desists.
There is nothing more.

Present Sense

There is only the moment
wedged between future and past,
            launched
with the significance of dust
toward a black hole oblivion.

Tear

In the reflection
of her tear,
I see myself
and cry.

DNA

Silence is as natural
and necessary as sound.
They are the DNA of music.

Water Drop

What is it like to be a drop of water?
A translucent raindrop born of a cloud
channeled along a gravity birth canal

an infinite procession of biological kin
raining down from sky or dripping from faucets,
changing form with insouciant ease

presiding in lakes and rivers, oceans and seas,
ponds and brooks, puddles and streams,
to nest at the heart of nourishment

for all animals, plants and fish —
a vital ingredient in all that is Earth,
absorbing elements like a fluent sponge

aware of historical eons predating genesis
where cognizant mortal-kind has not the final say.
Whether in solid stasis

or in crystal flight,
nature's clear liquid diet
the essence of life.

In Search of Existence

Did I know harmony before existence?
It mixes my baffled conscious
like ambiguities
badgering curiosity into action
on dreary, rainy days.

Is there destiny?
If so, why?
What end does she serve?
Has she favor for society's contributors
or are criminals and misfits included?

Am I to assimilate the landslide
of distorted, dismayed masses
entranced on surviving *this world*
in route to uncertainty?

Optimistic philosophy
lavished in time
and basked in wisdom
thrusts brilliant blue knowledge
gushers of understanding
and thunderous revelations
from opaque pits of obscurity,
balancing chaos and order
within a crimson goblet,
spilling few prophetic drops
into the infinite abundance
of dehydrated questions.

Home *is* the heart
of rock and mist.
Fear nothing;
love all,
life is balance
and all we do
embraces that goal.

Why are we here?

Bus Ride

She read the poetry
    I read
over my shoulder
    on the bus
much like I imagined
    myself
reciting it aloud
    in my mind.

I wonder if it sounded the same.

Married To the Muse

The Music of creativity:
breadcrumbs swirling in a gumbo
at the frantic feet of famished fowl.
Arrogant gestures of obnoxious prose
like a smoldering cigar
burn slowly at first,
gaining fiery momentum
with each ingratiating drag
blazing hybrid trails
of myriad images,
leading a naive conjurer
to a world of their own.

My Soul Remembers

My Soul remembers:
somnambulistic serenity in my mother's ambient
womb
my virgin awakening
my Spring cough
my inaugural breath
my commencement cry
my first delicate sop
my first glimmering glimpse
my embarkation sound
my first rickety step
arising, to fall,
arising, again
my first distinctive word
prefixed by an infant's laugh
my maiden song
my genesis poem
a teaspoon of this
a lollipop for that
accidents and forays
fairy tales and schemes
popsicles, candy and children's games
my first innocent kiss

my final passionate embrace
my first, first last first
since the beginning of the begin.

My Soul remembers:
fresh air, fresh fish, cool water and stale popcorn
the salty taste of my own sweat
bitter tears, boiling blood
dry spittle and vomit croquettes
textures and temperatures
aromas and scents
the variant flavors of passions intense
the clear steam of my lover's panting
ecstasy, deep and abysmal pain
volcanic climaxes and melodic wind chimes
sanctioned pleasures and sanctioned fruits
every wicked lie and lucid truth
each meandering fantasy
every rooted thought
a miraculous universe once an ink spot
Faustian nightmares and utopian dreams
a transcendental existence
in a metaphysical plane.

My Soul remembers:

       pharaohs, kings, paupers and queens
       wars, famine, pestilence and disease
       whips, chains, shackles and lynchings
       mothers, fathers, tribes and communities
       nations emblazoned in crimson glory
       countries erected on slavery and treason
       the whisper of thunder
       the roar of sunlight
       the symphony of water
       the dance of air
       tranquil sunrises over the body Sahara
       halcyon sunsets in the heart of Beijing
       when in God I did trust
       and The Almighty believed in me
       before His name existed
       before language came to be
       time before time awakened
       dispensing seconds which clip our lives -
       incarnation, reincarnation
       inner worlds and outer lives
       every moment of every moment
       before, during, after each delicious breath
       past, present, future and beyond.

My Soul remembers:
      so I am privileged to forget.

Pink Rose

A delicate pink rose
pressed flat
between satin-white pages
of a bound journal
at the bottom of a brown cardboard box
banished in the distant
dusty attic corner.
He had arrived on a cheerless autumn day
bearing such a gift
for the young woman of his dreams.
She thanked him
with a warm smile
that stilled his heart.
His discovery
would make a nice addition
to their fiftieth wedding anniversary celebration.

For My Sisters & Brothers in Verse

I know you, Sisters

not of the flesh, but in intellect —
your power, your grace, I have witnessed of late;
of past, of future, in time, out of time,
within a space as vast as our cosmos,
yet as minute as a refreshing drop of natural water
gathering thermodynamic power from its primal kinetic flow
gurgling, bubbling, rushing, tumbling, marauding into
a thunderous roar, a maddening crescendo of silken droplets
stretching out, collapsing in, changing shape and form
but never, not once, altering its fate;
permanent cores in the Golden Trunk of God.

I know you, Brothers —

your words, your rhythms pulse
in that pantheon within my naked vastness,
broken down, broken off, broken, only to be rebuilt
better, faster, stronger,
arresting concentric circles of hope — less — ness
manifesting myself through your genes
(or gems, if you'd allow me this claim?).

These are powerful seeds for fertile minds such as mine – field
to birth spry visions of life and paradigms of Hope
riding Death to its nebulous castle of bovine crypts.

You know me, Sisters.

You know me, Brothers.

As you have known Malcolm with an X and Martin who was King
Ashanti through Zulu and Apache through Zuni,
as you have known Greatness and it has come to know you
in its searing spotlight, in its miasma of shadows,
lurking, standing, crawling, peeking, whispering,
as you made aware to every echoing eardrum
capable of deciphering your drummer's code
or slap-'em-in-the-face message,
giving voice to the so-called power — less,
who ventured through
hovels, ghettoes, back roads, crossroads,
backwoods, alleys, dives, shacks,
honky-tonks, bars, speakeasies and juke joints,
your words, your messages tap-tap-tapping at our minds,
scratch-scratch-scratching at our souls.

You, Brothers, have known my body politics.

You, Sisters, have known my inner self,

before I could see my dreams. Before I could recognize my heart,
articulate my anguish, my oppression, my joys and my fury;
before I realized the meaning of those words
your adroit gifts slew my grim strife by reaffirming life
and fight and hope and doubt and fear cast out.

Brothers . . . Sisters,

so many questioning souls which you have anodized,
so many restive souls anodyne by your words,
on behalf of the myriad who have basked in your shared visions
I convey our immutable gratitude for eternity and beyond.

This Is Our Way

We file on public transportation
joining strange faces and foreign bodies,
a kindred throng.

A murder of humans in trance-like transit
compliant to earning a life,
no longer free as the day we were born.

Sharing weather, world, harmony and toil,
washed-out sightings to our murky visions,
garbled offerings to our imploded ears.

Modern zealots convince starving spirits
to claw with fervor at a capital dream.

"Why?" some minds whisper,
echoing without refrain or retort.

"Why not? Other minds assert,
echoing without refrain or retort.

Like dazed sheep, we wonder and wander,
wayward ghosts on a cyclic voyage

disembarking at STOP, after STOP, after *STOP* —
reflex, really; not conscious thought.

The "Whys" and "Why Nots,"
the perfumed and cologned,
the deodorized and street scented,

voracious microorganisms shuffling in the BIG dance
because we are informed –

and firmly believe —
that somebody's got to pay.

This is our way.

Paradise

This morning, I strolled to the shore
to watch the sunrise.
Dewy blue sky kissed a gentle emerald ocean
on a limpid horizon.
A bright red ball sat suspended
in the distance upon an invisible thread.
Seagulls glided near the edge of the world
echoing sentiments from God that all is well.
Cool copper sand formed grainy sandals
beneath my bare, chilly feet.
Water caressed the shore for a lover's moment
before returning home.
Damp salt breezes tingled my skin;
     all sounds seduced my mind.
        Paradise.
And through it all,
I longed for you.

Infinite Loves

If there are incalculable molecules
within a finite galaxy,
can there be
infinite loves
within one life,
one heart,
one soul?

Self Sacrifice

When winds cease
and liquid tear-shaped prisms fall
saturating our springy woolen curls,
tracing our skin slick limbs,
purging our individualism
          — will you come?

Will you faithfully relinquish,
without fear,
minus misgivings,
your threadbare soul
to the uncertain promise
          of us?

Human Contact

We have touched one another
as light touches images to eyes,
             a flash,
a frame of recognition,
             processed by brain cells
against previous experiences
             and original thoughts.

Infatuation

Her lips varied in motion,
apparently in speech,
curling at ends
displaying alabaster teeth,
while I listened
intrigued,
as a child engulfed in imaginative
telling of ancient Native legends
around a midnight campfire.
Her words eluded my ears.
Still I listened.
Her smile sparkled
in the cold, blue night,
sedating fixed brown eyes
like warm milk,
soothing my jittery tummy.

Longings

Out there,
    somewhere,
she waits,
    dissecting her life,
as I,
    pondering
who?
    when?
        how?
            if?
our destiny will happen.

Scripture

She asked me to explain why I love her.

I began my foolish answer quest
in the harbor of her pristine eyes,
moved to her beautiful face,
arrived at her stinging wit,
skipped to her sensuous body,
banked at her fiery temper,
tripped on her sultry tongue,
climbed along her motherland hair,
staggered through her brilliant mind,
hiked into her benevolent heart,
lapped at her natural spring,
settling in her tender soul.

Brightly wrapped honorable clichés
bearing sincere gifts
from my sandpaper lips,
attempting to bring into vivid focus
that which places her first in my affection,
not a solitary word articulated or muttered
at a crystal moment of ardent truth —
all be they summary facts! —
of her who I love.

Had I voiced what I profess
as bone marrow, unequivocal faith,
to my true Love's resounding "Why?"
In blunt, bold-face, honest honesty
I love you *because*
I love YOU.

This much I know...

The simple scripture of my soul.

The I Factor

A writer
sparked by the I Factor
scrambles to excite
cinders of possibilities.

Pen groping paper records:
characters
scenes
metaphors
action
similes
dialogue.

Thunder clouds
of reminiscences,
emotions,
moods,
swish violently through
his conscious filter.
Hasty attempts to transcribe
abstract piecemeal
into 3-D reality
disperse
dissolve

spear the heart
of his bright
gray light.

The fever breaks.
The writer is gutted
salvaging minute portions
of random wares
before most
flash to flames.

Blindly his search continues
until another door —
unexpectedly —
swoops open,
granting bantam peeks
at variant futures.

Notes

The first stanza for "My Soul Remembers" explores physical identity. The second stanza delves into sensual identity. The final stanza expands toward universal and spiritual awareness.

Acknowledgements

Thanks to the editors and staff of the following publications, living and deceased, where some of these offerings first found a home:

Ashes to Ashes, Poetry Press (Whirlpool)

More Big Thoughts, Golden Apple Press (DNA)

Secrets of a Blue-Green World, Golden Apple Press (Still We Laugh, Infatuation)

Loose Gravel, Vol. 1, No. 2 (The Screen)

The Armadillo Poetry Press Vol. 3, No. 3 (Infinite Loves)

The Armadillo Poetry Press Vol. 3, No. 2 (Paradise)

The Aurorean, Encircle Publications (Human Contact)

The Raintown Review: Poetry Edition, HarMona Press (Natural Evolution)

Michael R Lane was born and raised in Pittsburgh, Pennsylvania. Michael studied English Literature and Creative Writing at Point Park University, Sonoma State University, and Portland State University in an effort to hone his craft. He has written poetry for more than three decades, and has had poetry published in numerous journals.